Praying God's Words

Randy L Ballard

Thank you for choosing to pray God's words. Your prayer life is about ready to get a refreshing makeover. I am excited for you. I challenge you daily for a month to pray God's words. Before you do, please read the brief instructional articles. They will help prepare you to get all you can out of each day's prayer experience with the Lord. Now let's get started!

Copyright© 2019
All rights reserved

Scripture quotations marked NKJV are taken from the New King James Version. Copyright © 1982 by Randy L Ballard, Inc. Used by permission. All rights reserved.

Scripture quotations marked NLT are taken from the Holy Bible, New Living Translation copyright ©1966. Used by permission of Tyndale House Publishers, Inc. Wheaton, Illinois 60189. All rights reserved.

Visit www.relationaldiscipleshipministries.com for more information. Printed in the United States of America.

CONTENTS

Praying God's Words and the Prosperous Life

Twelve Tips for Praying God's Words

Benefits of Praying God's Words

Praying God's Words Over Your Children and Grandchildren

The Added Words in the Brackets

Praying God's Words for:

Day 1 - courage, protection, peace, rest, rescue - Psalm 3

Day 2 - direction, needs, praise, protection, worship - Psalm 5

Day 3 - direction, commitment, praise, protection, rest, worship - Psalm 16

Day 4 - blessings, nation, needs, praise, protection, success, worship – Psalm 20

Day 5 – trust, need, direction, strength, blessings, protection, forgiveness, praise and worship, Israel – Psalm 25

Day 6 - praise, health and healing, thanksgiving, deliverance, mercy, blessings, worship, favor – Psalm 30

Day 7 – forgiveness, protection, praise and worship, guidance - Psalm 32

Day 8 – needs, worship, deliverance, guidance, praise, protection – Psalm 40

Day 9 – discouragement, needs, worship, deliverance, guidance, praise, protection, hope – Psalm 43

Day 10 – forgiveness, personal purity, repentance, guilt, deliverance, guidance, praise, protection, joy, boldness – Psalm 51

Day 11 – rescue, repentance, deliverance, protection, brokenness – Psalm 55

Day 12 – victory, deliverance, hope, security, protection – Psalm 62

Day 13 - worship, praise, security – Psalm 63

Day 14 – praise, mercy justice, blessings – Psalm 67

Day 15 – trust, security, deliverance, hope, praise, strength, comfort, worship – Psalm 71

Day 16 – justice, the poor, orphans, the oppressed, the helpless – Psalm 82, worship, praise, strength, protection, provision – Psalm 84

Day 17 – forgiveness, restoration, salvation, truth, righteousness – Psalm 85

Day 18 – requests, protection, salvation, mercy, happiness, forgiveness, praise, deliverance, purity of heart, strength, comfort – Psalm 86

Day 19 – wisdom, presence, unfailing love, joy, gladness, his approval, success – Psalm 90

Day 20 – thanksgiving, praise, unfailing love, joy, growth/fruitfulness – Psalm 92

Day 21 – praise, thanksgiving, worship – Psalm 95 52

Day 22 – thanksgiving, praise, worship, the nations, Jesus' coming, justice – Psalm 96

Day 23 – praise, thanksgiving, worship, forgiveness, justice, unfailing love - Psalm 103

Day 24 – praise, obedience, children, success, generosity, trust – Psalm 112

Day 25 – praise, worship, poor, the childless – Psalm 113

Day 26 – praise, worship, Israel, a blessing over your children – Psalm 115

Day 27 – thanksgiving, in distress, help, strength, praise – Psalm 118

Day 28 – humility, simplicity in life, peace, contentment, trust, hope in the Lord – Psalm 131

Day 29 – self-examination, his presence, guidance, strength, thankfulness – Psalm 139

Day 30 – praise, spiritual warfare, protection, deliverance, children, prosperity, joy – Psalm 144

Day 31 – praise, his goodness, his compassion – Psalm 145

Praying God's Words and the Prosperous Life

"But they delight in the law of the LORD, meditating on it day and night. 3 They are like trees planted along the riverbank, bearing fruit each season. Their leaves never wither, and they prosper in all they do." - Psalm 1:2-3, NLT

7 "But blessed are those who trust in the LORD and have made the LORD their hope and confidence. 8 They are like trees planted along a riverbank, with roots that reach deep into the water. Such trees are not bothered by the heat or worried by long months of drought. Their leaves stay green, and they never stop producing fruit."
– Jeremiah 17:7, 8, NLT

7 "Be strong and very courageous. Be careful to obey all the instructions Moses gave you. Do not deviate from them, turning either to the right or to the left. Then you will be successful in everything you do. 8 Study this Book of Instruction continually. Meditate on it day and night so you will be sure to obey everything written in it. Only then will you prosper and succeed in all you do. 9 This is my command—be strong and courageous! Do not be afraid or discouraged. For the LORD your God is with you wherever you go." - Joshua 1:7-9, NLT

Twelve Tips for Praying God's Words

"Open the Bible, start reading it, and pause at every verse, and turn it into a prayer."
– John Piper

1. It's been my experience that the Psalms is easier to pray than other parts of the Bible. Therefore, most of the prayers in this book are from select passages from the Psalms. The Psalms speak directly to my life situation. The psalms were written by real people with real needs. Professor Don Whitney in his book, *Praying the Bible* suggests, "...as you read, you will experience their words becoming your words, and their hearts expressing your heart."

2. Read out loud line by line and talk to God about what you are reading or what you have just read.

3. If you don't understand the meaning of the verse, go on to the next one. If the meaning of that one is perfectly clear but nothing comes to mind to pray about, go on to the next one.

4. Let the scriptures "shape your prayers."

5. Don Whitney says to pray or talk to God about those thoughts that comes to your mind while reading or meditating on the scripture.

6. Let God initiate the conversation with you through the scriptures. You can respond with meditation, or praise, or with agreement or whatever is in your heart.

7. As you read, absorb God's words. You might choose a verse as you read that you want to commit to memory for that day. Write it out on a 3 x 5 card. Read over it.

Let it get down into your spirit. I like to say get it into the spiritual hard drive of your mind and heart. The Holy Spirit will draw it out when you need it.

8. Pray God's words over your children, grandchildren, spouse, neighbors, and brothers and sisters in Christ. Some Psalms are more suited for this than others.

9. When you come across verses that you can't figure out how to turn into a prayer, just skip it and move on to the next verse or passage of scripture. You might go back over it later and meditate on it while asking God to show you how to pray. Again, if nothing comes to mind, move on.

10. Philippians 4:6 says to "take every detail to the Lord in prayer" (JB Phillips Translation). So as you read and pray, leave nothing out. Every fear, every person, every worry, every situation, every relationship – everything means every little and big thing. God promises "peace that surpasses all understanding if we will practice taking every detail to Him in prayer with supplication and thanksgiving" (Philippians 4:7, emphasis added).

11. It's important to pray a translation that interprets the scriptures into your everyday conversation…words and phrases that you are acquainted with. For that reason, the passages in this book come from the NLT (New Living Translation) mostly. However, there are other good translations out there that you can pray from as well.

12. Doug Small, President and Founder of Alive Ministries, instructs intercessors "to wrestle with the scriptures in prayer."

Benefits of Praying God's Words

1. You will find yourself praying scriptural prayers rather than just making up your own prayers. Don Whitney says, "As you pray the text, you will experience the Spirit of God using the word of God to help the people of God pray increasingly according to the will of God." (I love that!)

2. It will be easier to continue in prayer. Your mind will wander less, and you will discover that you won't run out of things to say.

3. Jesus said, "the words that I have spoken to you are spirit and life" (John 6:63). When you pray God's words you pray spirit and life.

4. You will find that your prayers will be more God-centered and less self-centered. When our prayers consist more of God's attributes and who He is, it increases our faith and strength to face our own trials and temptations.

5. The scriptures will serve as a guide for you. I used the Lord's prayer when I was in my early 20's to go from praying 5 to 10 minutes to an hour a day. The Lord's prayer gave me a guide, a structure…it gave me topics in what to pray and how to pray.

6. It turns prayer into a true two-way conversation. You are praying to Him while He is talking with you. He is initiating the conversation and will speak as long as you want Him to.

7. You will find as you pray God's words you will retain more and find yourself meditating on it throughout your day.

8. You will discover that you have more confidence that you are praying the will of God.

9. Your prayer life will turn into an adventure, not just praying the same old things using the same old words. When you pray God's words, you will pray new things, using new words. You will pray for people and situations that you wouldn't think of on your own. Your prayers will be fresh, not redundant.

Praying God's Words Over Your Children

For example, a woman who prays for her children or grandchildren, could pray Psalm 23 over her children. Psalm 23 would transform her same old words to a dynamic new prayer enriched with inspired words.

Next day she might pray 1 Corinthians 13 over her children…that God might develop the agape love in her children/grandchildren. Isn't that a wonderful thing to do for your children and grandchildren?

Another time she might find herself in Galatians 5 praying the fruit of the spirit over them.

Another day, she might find herself in Psalm 139. Again, she would read over the following passage. Then she would begin to pray using the passage as a guide but praying with her own words.

7 I can never escape from your Spirit!
   I can never get away from your presence!
8 If I go up to heaven, you are there;
   if I go down to the grave, you are there.
9 If I ride the wings of the morning, if I dwell by the farthest oceans,
10 even there your hand will guide me, and your strength will support me.
11 I could ask the darkness to hide me
   and the light around me to become night—
12 but even in darkness I cannot hide from you.
   To you the night shines as bright as day.
   Darkness and light are the same to you.
13 You made all the delicate, inner parts of my body
   and knit me together in my mother's womb.
14 Thank you for making me so wonderfully complex! Your workmanship is marvelous—how well I know it.
15 You watched me as I was being formed in utter seclusion,
   as I was woven together in the dark of the womb.

[16] You saw me before I was born. Every day of my life was recorded in your book. Every moment was laid out before a single day had passed. [17] How precious are your thoughts about me, O God. They cannot be numbered!

Finally, Psalm 128 is great to pray over your children and grandchildren.

[1] How joyful are those who fear the LORD— all who follow his ways! [2] You will enjoy the fruit of your labor. How joyful and prosperous you will be! [3] Your wife will be like a fruitful grapevine, flourishing within your home. Your children will be like vigorous young olive trees as they sit around your table. [4] That is the LORD's blessing for those who fear him.

Praying God's Words

Prayers from the Psalms for each day of the Month

The Added Words in the Brackets

You will find as you pray through the Psalms in this book, I have added some pronouns (you, your, me, and I) to some of the passages to help you pray more personal prayers to the Lord. Of course, you do not have to use the words in the brackets. They are just there to assist you.

I should also explain that I have found the New Living Translation (NLT) to be the most helpful in praying God's words back to Him. The NLT is filled with the pronouns I, me, you, and your. In my own study time, I like to use many different translations. However, for praying the scriptures, I find the NLT the most helpful.

Finally, while praying try not to dwell too much on the words that are in the brackets. Ask the Holy Spirit to help you meditate on the passages and not be distracted. After praying through a passage once, go back and ponder over it line by line. Refuse to be in a hurry. Let the Holy Spirit illuminate God's words in you. Allow the Spirit to speak to you and you then converse with the Father. You might want to take some notes during this time so you can recall later the deep things of God.

This is intimate prayer…intimate worship of the Living God! These times are precious. They can be life changing…enriching, refreshing moments where you draw close to God and He draws close to you. These are times that you experience great oneness and intimacy with God as you are praying His heart.

Day 1

***PRAY GOD'S WORDS FOR:* PROTECTION, PEACE, COURAGE, REST, RESCUE**

Psalm 3

[1] O LORD, I have so many enemies;
  so many are against me.
[2] So many are saying,
  "God will never rescue him![me]" Interlude
[3] But you, O LORD, are a shield around me;
  you are my glory, the one who holds my head high.
[4] I cried out to the LORD,
  and he [You] answered me from his holy [Your] mountain. Interlude
[5] I lay down and slept,
  yet I woke up in safety,
  for the LORD was watching over me.
[6] I am not afraid of ten thousand enemies who surround me on every side.
[7] Arise, O LORD!
  Rescue me, my God!
  Slap all my enemies in the face! Shatter the teeth of the wicked!
[8] Victory comes from you, O LORD. May you bless your people.

Day 2

PRAY GOD'S WORDS FOR:
NEEDS, DIRECTION, PROTECTION, PRAISE & WORSHIP

Psalm 5

¹ O LORD, hear me as I pray; pay attention to my groaning.
² Listen to my cry for help, my King and my God, for I pray to no one but you.
³ Listen to my voice in the morning, LORD.
Each morning I bring my requests to you and wait expectantly.
⁴ O God, you take no pleasure in wickedness; you cannot tolerate the sins of the wicked.
⁵ Therefore, the proud may not stand in your presence, for you hate all who do evil.
⁶ You will destroy those who tell lies.
The LORD detests murderers and deceivers.
⁷ Because of your unfailing love, I can enter your house; I will worship at your Temple with deepest awe.
⁸ Lead me in the right path, O LORD, or my enemies will conquer me.
Make your way plain for me to follow. ⁹ ¹¹ But let all who take refuge in you rejoice;
let them sing joyful praises forever. Spread your protection over them,
that all who love your name may be filled with joy.
¹² For you bless the godly, O LORD;
you surround them with your shield of love.

Day 3

PRAY GOD'S WORDS FOR:
DIRECTION, REST, PROTECTION, PRAISE & WORSHIP, COMMITMENT

Psalm 16

1 Keep me safe, O God,
  for I have come to you for refuge.
2 I said to the LORD, "You are my Master!
  Every good thing I have comes from you."
3 The godly people in the land are my true heroes!
  I take pleasure in them!
4 Troubles multiply for those who chase after other gods.
  I will not take part in their sacrifices of blood or even speak
  the names of their gods.
5 LORD, you alone are my inheritance, my cup of blessing.
  You guard all that is mine.
6 The land you have given me is a pleasant land.
  What a wonderful inheritance!
7 I will bless the LORD who guides me;
  even at night my heart instructs me.
8 I know the LORD is [You are] always with me.
  I will not be shaken, for he is [You are] right beside me.
9 No wonder my heart is glad, and I rejoice.
  My body rests in safety.
10 For you will not leave my soul among the dead or allow your
  holy one to rot in the grave.
11 You will show me the way of life,
  granting me the joy of your presence
  and the pleasures of living with you forever.

Day 4

PRAY GOD'S WORDS FOR:
NEEDS, STRENGTH, BLESSINGS, SUCCESS, PROTECTION, PRAISE & WORSHIP, YOUR NATION

Psalm 20

1 In times of trouble, may the LORD answer your [my] cry. May the name of the God of Jacob keep you [me] safe from all harm.
2 May he send you [me] help from his sanctuary and strengthen you [me] from Jerusalem.
3 May he remember all your [my] gifts
and look favorably on your [my] burnt offerings.
Interlude
4 May he grant your [my] heart's desires
and make all your [my] plans succeed.
5 May we [I] shout for joy when we [I] hear of your victory and raise a victory banner in the name of our God.
May the LORD answer all your [my] prayers.

[Use the rest of the prayer to intercede for your nation's leaders and your nation.]

6 Now I know that the LORD rescues his anointed king.
He will answer him from his holy heaven and rescue him by his great power.
7 Some nations boast of their chariots and horses, but we boast in the name of the LORD our God.
8 Those nations will fall down and collapse, but we will rise up and stand firm.
9 Give victory to our king, O LORD!
Answer our cry for help.

Day 5

PRAY GOD'S WORDS FOR:
TRUST, NEEDS, DIRECTION, STRENGTH, BLESSINGS, PROTECTION, FORGIVENESS, PRAISE & WORSHIP, ISRAEL

Psalm 25

1 O LORD, I give my life to you.
2 I trust in you, my God!
   Do not let me be disgraced,
   or let my enemies rejoice in my defeat.
3 No one who trusts in you will ever be disgraced,
   but disgrace comes to those who try to deceive others.
4 Show me the right path, O LORD; point out the road for me to follow.
5 Lead me by your truth and teach me, for you are the God who saves me. All day long I put my hope in you.
6 Remember, O LORD, your compassion and unfailing love,
   which you have shown from long ages past.
7 Do not remember the rebellious sins of my youth. Remember me in the light of your unfailing love, for you are merciful, O LORD.
8 The LORD is good and does what is right;
   He shows the proper path to those who go astray.
9 He leads the humble in doing right, teaching them his way.
10 The LORD leads with unfailing love and faithfulness all who keep his covenant and obey His demands.
11 For the honor of your name, O LORD, forgive my many, many sins.
12 Who are those who fear the LORD?
   He [You] will show them [me] the path they [I[should choose.
13 They [I] will live in prosperity,
   and their [my] children will inherit the land.

14 The LORD is a friend to those who fear him.
   He teaches them His covenant.
15 My eyes are always on the LORD,
   for He rescues me from the traps of my enemies.
16 Turn to me and have mercy,
   for I am alone and in deep distress.
17 My problems go from bad to worse.
   Oh, save me from them all!
18 Feel my pain and see my trouble.
   Forgive all my sins.
19 See how many enemies I have and how viciously they hate me!
20 Protect me! Rescue my life from them!
   Do not let me be disgraced, for in you I take refuge.
21 May integrity and honesty protect me, for I put my hope in you.

[End by praying for the nation of Israel]

22 O God, ransom Israel
   from all its troubles

Day 6

PRAY GOD'S WORDS FOR:
PRAISE, HEALTH/HEALING, THANKSGIVING, DELIVERANCE, MERCY, BLESSINGS, WORSHIP, FAVOR

Psalm 30

1 I will exalt you, LORD, for you rescued me.
   You refused to let my enemies triumph over me.
2 O LORD my God, I cried to you for help, and you restored my
   health.
3 You brought me up from the grave, O LORD. You kept me
   from falling into the pit of death.
4 Sing to the LORD, all you godly ones!
   Praise his holy name.
5 For his anger lasts only a moment, but his favor lasts a
   lifetime!
   Weeping may last through the night, but joy comes with the
   morning.
6 When I was prosperous, I said,
   "Nothing can stop me now!"
7 Your favor, O LORD, made me as secure as a mountain. Then
   you turned away from me, and I was shattered.
8 I cried out to you, O LORD.
   I begged the LORD for mercy, saying,
9 "What will you gain if I die,
   if I sink into the grave? Can my dust praise you?
   Can it tell of your faithfulness?
10 Hear me, LORD, and have mercy on me.
   Help me, O LORD."
11 You have turned my mourning into joyful dancing. You have
   taken away my clothes of mourning and clothed me with joy,
12 that I might sing praises to you and not be silent. O LORD my
   God, I will give you thanks forever!

Day 7

PRAY GOD'S WORDS FOR: **FORGIVNESS, PROTECTION, PRAISE & WORSHIP, GUIDANCE**

Psalm 32

1 Oh, what joy for those
  whose disobedience is forgiven,
  whose sin is put out of sight!
2 Yes, what joy for those
  whose record the LORD has cleared of guilt, whose lives are
  lived in complete honesty!
3 When I refused to confess my sin, my body wasted away,
  and I groaned all day long.
4 Day and night your hand of discipline was heavy on me. My
  strength evaporated like water in the summer heat.
Interlude
5 Finally, I confessed all my sins to you and stopped trying to
  hide my guilt.
  I said to myself, "I will confess my rebellion to the
  LORD."
  And you forgave me! All my guilt is gone. *Interlude*
6 Therefore, let all the godly pray to you while there is still time,
  that they [we] may not drown in the floodwaters of judgment.
7 For you are my hiding place; you protect me from trouble.
  You surround me with songs of victory. *Interlude*
8 The LORD says, "I will guide you along the best pathway
  for your life. I will advise you and watch over you.
9 Do not be like a senseless horse or mule
  that needs a bit and bridle to keep it under control."
10 Many sorrows come to the wicked,
  but unfailing love surrounds those who trust the LORD.
11 So [I will] rejoice in the LORD and be glad, all you [we] who
  obey Him!
  Shout for joy, all you whose hearts are pure!

Day 8

PRAY GOD'S WORDS FOR:
NEEDS, WORSHIP, DELIVERANCE, GUIDANCE, PRAISE, PROTECTION

Psalm 40

¹ I waited patiently for the [You] LORD to help me, and he [You] turned to me and heard my cry.
² He [You] lifted me out of the pit of despair,
 out of the mud and the mire. He [You] set my feet on solid ground and steadied me as I walked along.
³ He [You have] has given me a new song to sing, a hymn of praise to our [my] God.
 Many will see what he [You LORD have] done and be amazed.
 They [I] will put their [my] trust in the LORD.
⁴ Oh, the joys of those who trust the LORD, who have no confidence in the proud
 or in those who worship idols.
⁵ O LORD my God, you have performed many wonders for us [me].
 Your plans for us [me] are too numerous to list. You have no equal.
 If I tried to recite all your wonderful deeds, I would never come to the end of them.
⁶ You take no delight in sacrifices or offerings.
 Now that you have made me listen, I finally understand—you don't require burnt offerings or sin offerings.
⁷ Then I said, "Look, I have come.
 As is written about me in the Scriptures:
⁸ I take joy in doing your will, my God,
 for your instructions are written on my heart."
⁹ I have told all your people about your justice. I have not been afraid to speak out,

as you, O LORD, well know.
10 I have not kept the good news of your justice hidden in my heart;
I have talked about your faithfulness and saving power.
I have told everyone in the great assembly of your unfailing love and faithfulness.
11 LORD, don't hold back your tender mercies from me.
Let your unfailing love and faithfulness always protect me.
12 For troubles surround me— too many to count!
My sins pile up so high
I can't see my way out.
They outnumber the hairs on my head.
I have lost all courage.
13 Please, LORD, rescue me!
Come quickly, LORD, and help me.
14 May those who try to destroy me be humiliated and put to shame.
May those who take delight in my trouble be turned back in disgrace.
15 Let them be horrified by their shame,
for they said, "Aha! We've got him now!"
16 But may all who search for you
be filled with joy and gladness in you.
May those who love your salvation
repeatedly shout, "The LORD is great!"
17 As for me, since I am poor and needy, let the LORD keep me in his thoughts.
You are my helper and my savior.
O my God, do not delay.

Day 9

PRAY GOD'S WORDS FOR: **DISCOURAGEMENT, NEEDS, WORSHIP, DELIVERANCE, GUIDANCE, PRAISE, PROTECTION, HOPE**

Psalm 43

[1] Declare me innocent, O God!
Defend me against these ungodly people. Rescue me from these unjust liars.
[2] For you are God, my only safe haven.
Why have you tossed me aside? Why must I wander around in grief,
oppressed by my enemies?
[3] Send out your light and your truth; let them guide me.
Let them lead me to your holy mountain, to the place where you live.
[4] There I will go to the altar of God, to God—the source of all my joy.
I will praise you with my harp, O God, my God!
[5] Why am I discouraged?
Why is my heart so sad?
I will put my hope in God!
I will praise him again—
my Savior and my God!

Day 10

PRAY GOD'S WORDS FOR: **FORGIVENESS, PERSONAL PURITY, REPENTANCE, GUILT, DELIVERANCE, GUIDANCE, PRAISE, PROTECTION, JOY, BROKENNESS**

Psalm 51

1 Have mercy on me, O God, because of your unfailing love.
   Because of your great compassion, blot out the stain of my sins.
2 Wash me clean from my guilt.
   Purify me from my sin.
3 For I recognize my rebellion; it haunts me day and night.
4 Against you, and you alone, have I sinned; I have done what is evil in your sight.
   You will be proved right in what you say, and your judgment against me is just.[a]
5 For I was born a sinner—
   yes, from the moment my mother conceived me.
6 But you desire honesty from the womb, teaching me wisdom even there.
7 Purify me from my sins, and I will be clean; wash me, and I will be whiter than snow.
8 Oh, give me back my joy again; you have broken me—
   now let me rejoice.
9 Don't keep looking at my sins.
   Remove the stain of my guilt.
10 Create in me a clean heart, O God.
   Renew a loyal spirit within me.
11 Do not banish me from your presence,
   and don't take your Holy Spirit from me.
12 Restore to me the joy of your salvation, and make me willing to obey you.

13 Then I will teach your ways to rebels, and they will return to you.
14 Forgive me for shedding blood, O God who saves; then I will joyfully sing of your forgiveness.
15 Unseal my lips, O LORD,
   that my mouth may praise you.
16 You do not desire a sacrifice, or I would offer one.
   You do not want a burnt offering.
17 The sacrifice you desire is a broken spirit.
   You will not reject a broken and repentant heart, O God.
18 Look with favor on Zion (Israel) and help her;

Day 11

PRAY GOD'S WORDS FOR:
RESCUE, REPENTANCE, DELIVERANCE, PROTECTION, BROKENNESS

Psalm 55

1 Listen to my prayer, O God.
   Do not ignore my cry for help!
2 Please listen and answer me,
   for I am overwhelmed by my troubles.
3 My enemies shout at me,
   making loud and wicked threats.
   They bring trouble on me and angrily hunt me down.
4 My heart pounds in my chest.
   The terror of death assaults me.
5 Fear and trembling overwhelm me, and I can't stop shaking.
6 Oh, that I had wings like a dove; then I would fly away and rest!
7 I would fly far away
   to the quiet of the wilderness. *Interlude*
8 How quickly I would escape—
   far from this wild storm of hatred.
9 Confuse them, LORD, and frustrate their plans, for I see
   violence and conflict in the city.
16 But I will call on (You) God,
   and the (you) LORD will rescue me.
17 Morning, noon, and night
   I cry out in my distress,
   and the LORD hears my voice.
18 He (You) ransom me and keep me safe from the battle waged
   against me, though many still oppose me.
19 God, who has ruled forever,
   (You) will hear me and humble them. *Interlude*
22 Give your burdens to the LORD, and he will take care of you.

He (You) will not permit the godly to slip and fall.
23 But you, O God, will send the wicked down to the pit of destruction.
Murderers and liars will die young, but I am trusting you to save me.

Day 12

PRAY GOD'S WORDS FOR:
VICTORY, DELIVERANCE, HOPE, SECURITY, PROTECTION

Psalm 62

¹ I wait quietly before God,
   for my victory comes from him [You].
² He [You] alone is [are] my rock and my salvation, my fortress
   where I will never be shaken.
³ So many enemies against one man— all of them trying to kill me.
   To them I'm just a broken-down wall or a tottering fence.
⁴ They plan to topple me from my high position.
   They delight in telling lies about me.
   They praise me to my face
   but curse me in their hearts. Interlude
⁵ Let all that I am wait quietly before God, for my hope is in him [You].
⁶ He [You] alone is [are] my rock and my salvation, my fortress
   where I will not be shaken.
⁷ My victory and honor come from God alone.
   He is [You are] my refuge, a rock where no enemy can reach me.
⁸ O my people, trust in him at all times.
   Pour out your heart to him,
   for God is our refuge. Interlude
¹¹ God has spoken plainly,
   and I have heard it many times: Power, O God, belongs to you;
¹² unfailing love, O LORD, is yours.
   Surely you repay all people according to what they have done.

Day 13

PRAY GOD'S WORDS FOR:
WORSHIP, PRAISE, SECURITY

Psalm 63

1 O God, you are my God;
   I earnestly search for you.
   My soul thirsts for you;
   my whole body longs for you in this parched and weary land where there is no water.
2 I have seen you in your sanctuary
   and gazed upon your power and glory.
3 Your unfailing love is better than life itself; how I praise you!
4 I will praise you as long as I live, lifting up my hands to you in prayer.
5 You satisfy me more than the richest feast.
   I will praise you with songs of joy.
6 I lie awake thinking of you, meditating on you through the night.
7 Because you are my helper,
   I sing for joy in the shadow of your wings.
8 I cling to you;
   your strong right hand holds me securely.

Day 14

PRAY GOD'S WORDS FOR:
FOR THE NATIONS, PRAISE, MERCY, BLESSING, JUSTICE

Psalm 67

God be merciful to us and bless us,
And cause His [Your] face to shine upon us, *Selah*
2 That Your way may be known on earth, Your salvation among all nations.
3 Let the peoples praise You, O God; Let all the peoples praise You.
4 Oh, let the nations be glad and sing for joy! For You shall judge the people righteously, And govern the nations on earth. *Selah*
5 Let the peoples praise You, O God; Let all the peoples praise You.
6 *Then* the earth shall yield her increase; God, our own God, shall bless us.
7 God shall bless us,
And all the ends of the earth shall fear Him [You].

Day 15

PRAY GOD'S WORDS FOR:
TRUST, SECURITY, DELIVERANCE, HOPE, PRAISE, STRENGTH, COMFORT, WORSHIP

Psalm 71

1 In You, O LORD, I put my trust; Let me never be put to shame.
2 Deliver me in Your righteousness, and cause me to escape;
   Incline Your ear to me, and save me.
3 Be my strong refuge,
   To which I may resort continually;
   You have given the commandment to save me, For You *are* my rock and my fortress.
4 Deliver me, O my God, out of the hand of the wicked, Out of the hand of the unrighteous and cruel man.
5 For You are my hope, O LORD GOD;
   You are my trust from my youth.
6 By You I have been upheld from birth;
   You are He who took me out of my mother's womb.
   My praise *shall be* continually of You. 7 I have become as a wonder to many, But You *are* my strong refuge.
8 Let my mouth be filled *with* Your praise
   And with Your glory all the day.
9 Do not cast me off in the time of old age; Do not forsake me when my strength fails. 10 For my enemies speak against me;
   And those who lie in wait for my life take counsel together,
11 Saying, "God has forsaken him;
   Pursue and take him, for *there is* none to deliver *him.*"
12 O God, do not be far from me;
   O my God, make haste to help me!
13 Let them be confounded *and* consumed Who are adversaries of my life;

Let them be covered *with* reproach and dishonor Who seek my hurt.
14 But I will hope continually,
And will praise You yet more and more.
15 My mouth shall tell of Your righteousness
And Your salvation all the day, For I do not know *their* limits.
16 I will go in the strength of the LORD GOD;
I will make mention of Your righteousness, of Yours only.
17 O God, You have taught me from my youth; And to this *day* I declare Your wondrous works. 18 Now also when *I am* old and gray headed,
O God, do not forsake me,
Until I declare Your strength to *this* generation, Your power to everyone *who* is to come.
19 Also Your righteousness, O God, *is* very high, You who have done great things;
O God, who *is* like You?
20 *You,* who have shown me great and severe troubles, Shall revive me again,
And bring me up again from the depths of the earth.
21 You shall increase my greatness, And comfort me on every side.
22 Also with the lute I will praise You—
And Your faithfulness, O my God! To You I will sing with the harp, O Holy One of Israel.
23 My lips shall greatly rejoice when I sing to You, And my soul, which You have redeemed.
24 My tongue also shall talk of Your righteousness all the day long;
For they are confounded,
For they are brought to shame
Who seek my hurt.

Day 16

PRAY GOD'S WORDS FOR:
JUSTICE, THE POOR, ORPHANS, THE OPPRESSED AND THE HELPLESS

Psalm 82

³ "Give justice to the poor and the orphan;
 uphold the rights of the oppressed and the destitute.
⁴ Rescue the poor and helpless;
 deliver them from the grasp of evil people Rise up, O God,
 and judge the earth,
 for all the nations belong to you.

PRAY GOD'S WORDS FOR:
WORSHIP, PRAISE, STRENGTH, PROTECTION, PROVISION

Psalm 84

¹ How lovely *is* Your tabernacle, O LORD of hosts!
² My soul longs, yes, even faints For the courts of the LORD;
 My heart and my flesh cry out for the living God.
³ Even the sparrow has found a home, And the swallow a nest for herself, Where she may lay her young— *Even* Your altars, O LORD of hosts, My King and my God.
⁴ Blessed *are* those who dwell in Your house; They will still be praising You. Selah
⁵ Blessed *is* the man whose strength *is* in You, Whose heart *is* set on pilgrimage.
⁶ *As they* pass through the Valley of Baca, They make it a spring;
 The rain also covers it with pools.
⁷ They go from strength to strength;
 Each one appears before God in Zion.

⁸ O LORD God of hosts, hear my prayer; Give ear, O God of
Jacob! Selah
⁹ O God, behold our shield,
And look upon the face of Your anointed.
¹⁰ For a day in Your courts *is* better than a thousand.
I would rather be a doorkeeper in the house of my God Than
dwell in the tents of wickedness.
¹¹ For the LORD God *is* a sun and shield; The LORD will give
grace and glory; No good *thing* will He withhold
From those who walk uprightly.
¹² O LORD of hosts,
Blessed *is* the man who trusts in You!

Day 17

***PRAY GOD'S WORDS FOR:* FORGIVENESS, RESTORATION, SALVATION, TRUTH, RIGHTEOUSNESS**

Psalm 85

¹ LORD, you poured out blessings on your land!
    You restored the fortunes of Israel.
² You forgave the guilt of your people— yes, you covered all
    their sins. Interlude
³ You held back your fury.
    You kept back your blazing anger.
⁴ Now restore us again, O God of our salvation.
    Put aside your anger against us once more.
⁵ Will you be angry with us always?
    Will you prolong your wrath to all generations?
⁶ Won't you revive us again,
    so your people can rejoice in you?
⁷ Show us your unfailing love, O LORD, and grant us your
    salvation.
⁸ I listen carefully to what God the LORD is saying, for he
    speaks peace to his faithful people.
    But let them not return to their foolish ways.
⁹ Surely his salvation is near to those who fear him, so our land
    will be filled with his glory.
¹⁰ Unfailing love and truth have met together.
    Righteousness and peace have kissed!
¹¹ Truth springs up from the earth,
    and righteousness smiles down from heaven.
¹² Yes, the LORD pours down his blessings. Our land will yield
    its bountiful harvest.
¹³ Righteousness goes as a herald before him,
    preparing the way for his steps

Day 18

PRAY GOD'S WORDS FOR:
REQUESTS, PROTECTION, SALVATION, MERCY, HAPPINESS, FORGIVENESS, PRAISE, DELIVERANCE, PURITY OF HEART, STRENGTH, COMFORT

Psalm 86

[1] Bend down, O LORD, and hear my prayer; answer me, for I need your help.
[2] Protect me, for I am devoted to you.
    Save me, for I serve you and trust you. You are my God.
[3] Be merciful to me, O LORD,
    for I am calling on you constantly.
[4] Give me happiness, O LORD, for I give myself to you.
[5] O LORD, you are so good, so ready to forgive,
    so full of unfailing love for all who ask for your help.
[6] Listen closely to my prayer, O LORD; hear my urgent cry.
[7] I will call to you whenever I'm in trouble,
    and you will answer me.
[8] No pagan god is like you, O LORD.
    None can do what you do!
[9] All the nations you made
    will come and bow before you, LORD; they will praise your holy name.
[10] For you are great and perform wonderful deeds.
    You alone are God.
[11] Teach me your ways, O LORD,
    that I may live according to your truth!
    Grant me purity of heart, so that I may honor you.
[12] With all my heart I will praise you, O LORD my God.
    I will give glory to your name forever,
[13] for your love for me is very great.
    You have rescued me from the depths of death.

¹⁴ O God, insolent people rise up against me; a violent gang is trying to kill me.
You mean nothing to them.
¹⁵ But you, O LORD,
are a God of compassion and mercy, slow to get angry
and filled with unfailing love and faithfulness.
¹⁶ Look down and have mercy on me. Give your strength to your servant;
save me, the son (or daughter) of your servant.
¹⁷ Send me a sign of your favor.
Then those who hate me will be put to shame, for you, O LORD, help and comfort me.

Day 19

PRAY GOD'S WORDS FOR:
WISDOM, HIS PRESENCE, HIS UNFAILING LOVE, JOY, GLADNESS, HIS APPROVAL, SUCCESS

Psalm 90

¹ LORD, through all the generations you have been our home!
² Before the mountains were born,
   before you gave birth to the earth and the world, from beginning to end, you are God.
³ You turn people back to dust, saying,
   "Return to dust, you mortals!"
⁴ For you, a thousand years are as a passing day, as brief as a few night hours.
⁵ You sweep people away like dreams that disappear. They are like grass that springs up in the morning.
⁶ In the morning it blooms and flourishes, but by evening it is dry and withered.
⁷ We wither beneath your anger;
   we are overwhelmed by your fury.
⁸ You spread out our sins before you— our secret sins—and you see them all.
⁹ We live our lives beneath your wrath, ending our years with a groan.
¹⁰ Seventy years are given to us!
   Some even live to eighty.
   But even the best years are filled with pain and trouble; soon they disappear, and we fly away.
¹¹ Who can comprehend the power of your anger?
   Your wrath is as awesome as the fear you deserve.
¹² Teach us to realize the brevity of life, so that we may grow in wisdom.
¹³ O LORD, come back to us! How long will you delay? Take pity on your servants!

¹⁴ Satisfy us each morning with your unfailing love, so we may sing for joy to the end of our lives.
¹⁵ Give us gladness in proportion to our former misery!
Replace the evil years with good.
¹⁶ Let us, your servants, see you work again; let our children see your glory.
¹⁷ And may the LORD our God show us his approval and make our efforts successful.
Yes, make our efforts successful!

Day 20

PRAY GOD'S WORDS FOR:
THANKSGIVING, PRAISE, HIS UNFAILING LOVE, JOY, GROWTH/FRUITFULNESS

Psalm 92

1 It is good to give thanks to the LORD, to sing praises to the Most High.
2 It is good to proclaim your unfailing love in the morning, your faithfulness in the evening,
3 accompanied by a ten-stringed instrument, a harp, and the melody of a lyre.
4 You thrill me, LORD, with all you have done for me!
I sing for joy because of what you have done.
5 O LORD, what great works you do! And how deep are your thoughts.
6 Only a simpleton would not know,
and only a fool would not understand this:
7 Though the wicked sprout like weeds and evildoers flourish, they will be destroyed forever.
8 But you, O LORD, will be exalted forever.
9 Your enemies, LORD, will surely perish; all evildoers will be scattered.
10 But you have made me as strong as a wild ox.
You have anointed me with the finest oil.
11 My eyes have seen the downfall of my enemies;
my ears have heard the defeat of my wicked opponents.
12 But the godly will flourish like palm trees and grow strong like the cedars of Lebanon.
13 For they are [I am] transplanted to [in] the LORD's own house.
They [I will] flourish in the courts of our God.
14 Even in old age they [I] will still produce fruit; they [and I] will remain vital and green.

15 They [I] will declare, "The LORD is just!
   He is [You are] my rock! There is no evil in him [You]!"

Day 21

PRAY GOD'S WORDS FOR: **PRAISE, THANKSGIVING, WORSHIP**

Psalm 95

¹ Oh come, let us sing to the LORD!
  Let us shout joyfully to the Rock of our salvation.
² Let us come before His presence with thanksgiving; Let us shout joyfully to Him with psalms.
³ For the LORD *is* the great God,
  And the great King above all gods.
⁴ In His hand *are* the deep places of the earth; The heights of the hills *are* His also.
⁵ The sea *is* His, for He made it; And His hands formed the dry *land.*
⁶ Oh come, let us worship and bow down; Let us kneel before the LORD our Maker. ⁷ For He *is* our God,
  And we *are* the people of His pasture, And the sheep of His hand.

Day 22

***PRAY GOD'S WORDS FOR:* THANKSGIVING, PRAISE, WORSHIP, THE NATIONS, HIS COING, JUSTICE**

Psalm 96

1 [I will] Sing a new song to the LORD! Let the whole earth sing to the LORD!
2 [I will] Sing to the LORD; [I will] praise His name.
Each day [I will] proclaim the good news that He saves.
3 [I will] Publish His [Your] glorious deeds among the nations.
[I will] Tell everyone about the amazing things [You do] He does.
4 Great is the LORD! He is [You are] most worthy of praise!
He is [You are] to be feared above all gods.
5 The gods of other nations are mere idols, but the [You] LORD made the heavens!
6 Honor and majesty surround [You] Him; strength and beauty fill His [Your] sanctuary.
7 O nations of the world, recognize the LORD; recognize that the LORD is glorious and strong.
8 Give to the LORD the glory He deserves! Bring your offering and come into His courts.
9 Worship the LORD in all his holy splendor.
Let all the earth tremble before him.
10 Tell all the nations, "The LORD reigns!"
The world stands firm and cannot be shaken. He will judge all peoples fairly.
11 Let the heavens be glad, and the earth rejoice!
Let the sea and everything in it shout His praise!
12 Let the fields and their crops burst out with joy!
Let the trees of the forest sing for joy
13 before the LORD, for He is [You are] coming!
He is [You are] coming to judge the earth.

He [You will] will judge the world with justice, and the nations with His [Your] truth.

Day 23

PRAY GOD'S WORDS FOR:
PRAISE, THANKSGIVING, WORSHIP, FORGIVENESS, JUSTICE, UNFAILING LOVE

Psalm 103

1 Let all that I am praise the LORD;
   with my whole heart, I will praise his holy name.
2 Let all that I am praise the LORD;
   may I never forget the good things he does [You do] for me.
3 He forgives [You forgive] all my sins and heals all my diseases.
4 He redeems [You redeem] me from death
   and crowns [crown] me with love and tender mercies.
5 He fills [You fill] my life with good things.
   My youth is renewed like the eagle's!
6 The LORD gives [me] righteousness
   and justice to all who are treated unfairly.
7 He revealed his character to Moses and his deeds to the people of Israel.
8 The LORD is compassionate and merciful,
   slow to get angry and filled with unfailing love.
9 He [You] will not constantly accuse us [me], nor remain angry forever.
10 He does [You will] not punish us for all our sins; he does [You will] not deal harshly with us, as we deserve.
11 For his [You have] unfailing love toward those who fear him [You] is as great as the height of the heavens above the earth.
12 He has [You LORD have] removed our sins as far from us as the east is from the west.
13 The LORD is like a father to his children,
   tender and compassionate to those who fear him.
14 For he [You] knows how weak we are;
   he remembers [You remember] we are only dust.

15 Our [my] days on earth are like grass; like wildflowers, we bloom and die.
16 The wind blows, and we are gone— as though we had never been here.
17 But the love of the LORD remains forever with those who fear him.
His [Your] salvation extends to the children's children
18 of those who are faithful to his covenant,
of those who obey his [Your] commandments!
19 The LORD has made the heavens his throne; from there he rules over everything.
20 Praise the LORD, you angels,
you mighty ones who carry out his plans, listening for each of his commands.
21 Yes, praise the LORD, you armies of angels who serve him and do his will!
22 Praise the LORD, everything he has created, everything in all his kingdom.
Let all that I am praise the LORD.

Day 24

***PRAY GOD'S WORDS FOR:* PRAISE, JOY, OBEDIENCE, CHILDREN, SUCCESS, GENEROSITY, TRUST**

Psalm 112

Praise the LORD!
How joyful are those who fear the LORD and delight in obeying his commands.
2 Their children will be successful everywhere;
    an entire generation of godly people will be blessed.
3 They themselves will be wealthy,
    and their good deeds will last forever.
4 Light shines in the darkness for the godly.
    They are generous, compassionate, and righteous.
5 Good comes to those who lend money generously and conduct
    their business fairly.
6 Such people will not be overcome by evil.
    Those who are righteous will be long remembered.
7 They do not fear bad news;
    they confidently trust the LORD to care for them.
8 They are confident and fearless
    and can face their foes triumphantly.
9 They share freely and give generously to those in need.
    Their good deeds will be remembered forever. They will have influence and honor.

Day 25

PRAY GOD'S WORDS FOR:
PRAISE, WORSHIP, POOR, THE CHILDLESS

Psalm 113

¹ Praise the LORD! Yes, give praise [let's give praise], O servants of the LORD. Praise the name of the LORD!
² Blessed be the name of the LORD now and forever.
³ Everywhere—from east to west—
praise [I will praise] the name of the LORD.
⁴ For the LORD is high above the nations;
his [your] glory is higher than the heavens.
⁵ Who can be compared with the LORD our God, who is enthroned on high?
⁶ He stoops [You stoop] to look down on heaven and on earth.
⁷ He lifts [You lift] the poor from the dust and the needy from the garbage dump.
⁸ He sets [You set] them among princes,
even the princes of his [Your] own people!
⁹ He gives [You give] the childless woman a family, making her a happy mother.

Praise   the   Lord!

Day 26

PRAY GOD'S WORDS FOR:
PRAISE, WORSHIP, ISRAEL, A BLESSING OVER YOUR CHILDREN,

Psalm 115

¹ Not to us, O LORD, not to us,
   but to your name goes all the glory
   for your unfailing love and faithfulness.
² Why let the nations say,
   "Where is their God?"
³ Our God is in the heavens, and he does as he wishes.
⁴ Their idols are merely things of silver and gold, shaped by
   human hands.
⁵ They have mouths but cannot speak, and eyes but cannot see.
⁶ They have ears but cannot hear, and noses but cannot smell.
⁷ They have hands but cannot feel, and feet but cannot walk,
   and throats but cannot make a sound.
⁸ And those who make idols are just like them, as are all who
   trust in them.
⁹ O Israel, trust the LORD!
   He is your helper and your shield.
¹⁰ O priests, descendants of Aaron, trust the LORD!
   He is your helper and your shield.
¹¹ All you who fear the LORD, trust the LORD!
   He is your helper and your shield.
¹² The LORD remembers us and will bless us.
   He will bless the people of Israel
   and bless the priests, the descendants of Aaron.
¹³ He will bless those who fear the LORD, both great and lowly.
¹⁴ May the LORD richly bless
   both you and your children.
¹⁵ May you be blessed by the LORD, who made heaven and
   earth.

¹⁶ The heavens belong to the Lord,
   but He has given the earth to all humanity.
¹⁷ The dead cannot sing praises to the Lord,
   for they have gone into the silence of the grave.
¹⁸ But we can praise the Lord both now and forever!

Praise   the   Lord!

Day 27

***PRAY GOD'S WORDS FOR:* THANKSGIVING, IN DISTRESS, HELP, STRENGTH, PRAISE**

Psalm 118

¹ Oh, give thanks to the LORD, for *He is* [You are] good! For His [Your] mercy *endures* forever. ² Let Israel now say, "His mercy *endures* forever."
³ Let the house of Aaron now say,
 "His mercy *endures* forever."
⁴ Let those who fear the LORD now say,
 "His mercy *endures* forever." ⁵ I called on the LORD in distress; The LORD answered me *and set me* in a broad place.
⁶ The LORD *is* on my side; I will not fear.
 What can man do to me?
⁷ The LORD is for me among those who help me; Therefore I shall see *my desire* on those who hate me. ⁸ *It is* better to trust in the LORD
 Than to put confidence in man.
⁹ *It is* better to trust in the LORD Than to put confidence in princes. ¹⁰ All nations surrounded me,
 But in the name of the LORD I will destroy them.
¹¹ They surrounded me, Yes, they surrounded me;
 But in the name of the LORD I will destroy them.
¹² They surrounded me like bees;
 They were quenched like a fire of thorns;
 For in the name of the LORD I will destroy them.
¹³ You pushed me violently, that I might fall, But the LORD helped me.
¹⁴ The LORD *is* my strength and song, And He has become my salvation.
¹⁵ The voice of rejoicing and salvation
 Is in the tents of the righteous;

The right hand of the LORD does valiantly. [16] The right hand of the LORD is exalted; The right hand of the LORD does valiantly. [17] I shall not die, but live,
And declare the works of the LORD.
[18] The LORD has chastened me severely, But He has not given me over to death.

PRAY DAILY...

[19] Open to me the gates of righteousness; I will go through them,
And I will praise the LORD.
[20] This is the gate of the LORD,
Through which the righteous shall enter.
[21] I will praise You,
For You have answered me, And have become my salvation.
[22] The stone *which* the builders rejected Has become the chief cornerstone.
[23] This was the LORD's doing;
It *is* marvelous in our eyes.
[24] This *is* the day the LORD has made; We will rejoice and be glad in it.
[25] Save now, I pray, O LORD;
O LORD, I pray, send now prosperity.
[26] Blessed *is* he who comes in the name of the LORD! We have blessed you from the house of the LORD.
[27] God *is* the LORD,
And He has given us light;
Bind the sacrifice with cords to the horns of the altar.
[28] You *are* my God, and I will praise You;
You are my God, I will exalt You.
[29] Oh, give thanks to the LORD, for *He is* good! For His mercy *endures* forever.

Day 28

PRAY GOD'S WORDS FOR:
HUMILITY, SIMPLICITY IN LIFE, PEACE, CONTENTMENT, TRUST, HOPE IN THE LORD

Psalm 131

1 LORD, my heart is not proud; my eyes are not haughty.
   I don't concern myself with matters too great
   or too awesome for me to grasp.
2 Instead, I have calmed and quieted myself,
   like a weaned child who no longer cries for its mother's milk.
   Yes, like a weaned child is my soul within me.
3 O Israel, put your hope in the LORD—
   now and always. [Pray for the church and Israel here]

Day 29

***PRAY GOD'S WORDS FOR:* SELF-EXAMINATION, HIS PRESENCE, GUIDANCE, STRENGTH, THANKFULNESS**

Psalm 139

1 O LORD, you have examined my heart and know everything about me.
2 You know when I sit down or stand up.
  You know my thoughts even when I'm far away.
3 You see me when I travel and when I rest at home. You know everything I do.
4 You know what I am going to say even before I say it, LORD.
5 You go before me and follow me.
  You place your hand of blessing on my head.
6 Such knowledge is too wonderful for me, too great for me to understand!
7 I can never escape from your Spirit!
  I can never get away from your presence!
8 If I go up to heaven, you are there;
  if I go down to the grave, you are there.
9 If I ride the wings of the morning, if I dwell by the farthest oceans,
10 even there your hand will guide me, and your strength will support me.
11 I could ask the darkness to hide me
  and the light around me to become night—
12 but even in darkness I cannot hide from you. To you the night shines as bright as day.
  Darkness and light are the same to you.
13 You made all the delicate, inner parts of my body
  and knit me together in my mother's womb.
14 Thank you for making me so wonderfully complex!
  Your workmanship is marvelous—how well I know it.

15 You watched me as I was being formed in utter seclusion, as I was woven together in the dark of the womb.
16 You saw me before I was born.
Every day of my life was recorded in your book.
Every moment was laid out before a single day had passed.
17 How precious are your thoughts about me, O God.
They cannot be numbered!
18 I can't even count them;
they outnumber the grains of sand!
And when I wake up, you are still with me!
[verses 19-22 may not be prayable passages]
23 Search me, O God, and know my heart; test me and know my anxious thoughts.
24 Point out anything in me that offends you, and lead me along the path of everlasting life.

Day 30

***PRAY GOD'S WORDS FOR:* PRAISE, SPIRITUAL WARFARE, PROTECTION, DELIVERANCE, CHILDREN, PROSPERITY, JOY**

Psalm 144

¹ Praise the LORD, who is my rock.
   He trains [You train] my hands for war and gives my fingers skill for battle.
² He is [You are] my loving ally and my fortress, my tower of safety, my rescuer.
   He is [You are] my shield, and I take refuge in him [You].
   He [You] make the nations submit to me.
³ O LORD, what are human beings that you should notice them,
   mere mortals that you should think about them?
⁴ For they are like a breath of air;
   their days are like a passing shadow.
⁵ Open the heavens, LORD, and come down.
   Touch the mountains so they billow smoke.
⁶ Hurl your lightning bolts and scatter your enemies!
   Shoot your arrows and confuse them!
⁷ Reach down from heaven and rescue me; rescue me from deep waters,
   from the power of my enemies.
⁸ Their mouths are full of lies;
   they swear to tell the truth, but they lie instead.
⁹ I will sing a new song to you, O God!
   I will sing your praises with a ten-stringed harp.
¹⁰ For you grant victory to kings!
   You rescued your servant David from the fatal sword.
¹¹ Save me!
   Rescue me from the power of my enemies. Their mouths are full of lies;
   they swear to tell the truth, but they lie instead.

¹² May our sons flourish in their youth like well-nurtured plants.
May our daughters be like graceful pillars, carved to beautify a palace.
¹³ May our barns be filled with crops of every kind.
May the flocks in our fields multiply by the thousands, even tens of thousands,
¹⁴ and may our oxen be loaded down with produce. May there be no enemy breaking through our walls, no going into captivity,
no cries of alarm in our town squares.
¹⁵ Yes, joyful are those who live like this!
Joyful indeed are those whose God is the LORD.

Day 31

PRAY GOD'S WORDS FOR: PRAISE, HIS GOODNESS, HIS COMPASSION

Psalm 145

¹ I will exalt you, my God and King,
   and praise your name forever and ever.
² I will praise you every day; yes, I will praise you forever.
³ Great is the LORD! (You are) most worthy of praise!
   No one can measure (Your) greatness.
⁴ Let each generation tell its children of your mighty acts; let them proclaim your power.
⁵ I will meditate on your majestic, glorious splendor and your wonderful miracles.
⁶ Your awe-inspiring deeds will be on every tongue; I will proclaim your greatness.
⁷ Everyone will share the story of your wonderful goodness;
   they will sing with joy about your righteousness.
⁸ The LORD is merciful and compassionate,
   slow to get angry and filled with unfailing love.
⁹ The LORD is good to everyone.
   He showers compassion on all his creation.
¹⁰ All of your works will thank you, LORD, and your faithful followers will praise you.
¹¹ They will speak of the glory of your kingdom; they will give examples of your power.
¹² They will tell about your mighty deeds
   and about the majesty and glory of your reign.
¹³ For your kingdom is an everlasting kingdom.
   You rule throughout all generations.
   LORD (YOU) always keeps (your) promises; (You are) gracious in all (You do).
¹⁴ The LORD helps the fallen
   and lifts those bent beneath their loads.

¹⁵ The eyes of all look to you in hope;
   you give them their food as they need it.
¹⁶ When you open your hand,
   you satisfy the hunger and thirst of every living thing.
¹⁷ LORD (You are) righteous in everything (You do); (You are) filled with kindness.
¹⁸ LORD (You are) close to all who call on (You), yes, to all who call on (You) in truth.
¹⁹ (You grant) the desires of those who fear (You); (You) hear the cries for help and rescues them.
²⁰ LORD (You) protect all those who love (You), but (You) destroy the wicked.
²¹ I will praise (You) LORD,
   and may everyone on earth bless (Your) holy name forever and ever.

BIBLIOGRAPHY

- Don Whitney, *Praying the Bible*, (Wheaton, IL., Crossway Publishing, 2015).